My First Book About Frogs

Amazing Animal Books Children's Picture Books

by John Davidson

Mendon Cottage Books

JD-Biz Publishing

Read More Amazing Animal Books

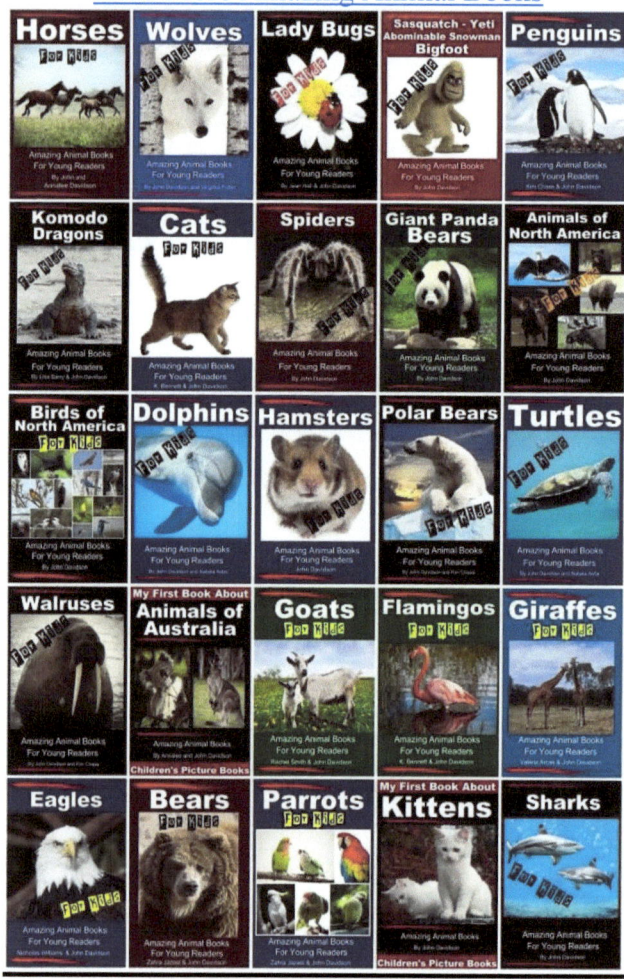

Purchase at Amazon.com

Download Free Books!
http://MendonCottageBooks.com

Table of Contents

Frogs

Wherever you are, wherever you live…you will find frogs!
These little guys live all over the world, except in Antarctica.

Red Poison Dart Frog

Frogs often turn into handsome men and beautiful princesses
in fairy tales.

Chinese legend links frogs with magicians. In Scotland, you give pictures of them as gifts to new neighbors.

Fascinating Facts

1. There are about 3,900 different types of frogs, including toads.

2. All frogs have flat heads, bulging eyes and big back legs.

Azure dart frog

3. Toads usually have warty, rough skins and are often poisonous.

4. Frogs do not need to drink water because they can absorb it through their skin.

5. Frogs swallow their food whole.

6. Frogs like coming out when it's wet, especially after it has just rained.

Green Pond Frog

7. Frogs do not see colors; they only see black and white.

8. Frogs only live in fresh water.

The Frog's Life Cycle

Eggs

Frogs first begin as eggs. The female frog will lay about 3,000 eggs and only 3-5 of those will usually survive.

Toads mating

The eggs are usually laid in a calm stretch of water and they will stick together and create a layer of protective foam.

Eggs hatch into tadpoles around 7 to 21 days after being laid.

Tadpoles

A tadpole only has a mouth, a tail, bad gills and is very fragile.

It takes the tadpole 4 weeks to develop better gills that are covered by a thin skin.

Common Frog tadpole

After 6 to 9 weeks, the tadpole will get a better head, grow long legs, and have a longer body.

Froglets

At 9-12 weeks, the young frog looks a lot like an adult but they still have a tail.

Froglet

They will now start to leave the water for adventures on land.

Adult Frogs

By the time it is between 12 to 16 weeks, the frog is fully grown.

It no longer has a tail, and it will have strong back legs, shorter arms, and a loud voice.

The Great Tree Frog

Life span

Frogs usually live between 3 – 17 years; with the oldest frog living to be a whopping 40 years!

Where Do Frogs Live?

Frogs can live on land and in the water.

Frogs actually live all over the world except for in the very coldest and hottest places.

Frog in a pond

Hibernation

Frogs are cold blooded, so when it gets very cold, frogs go into hibernation.

Toad

What is hibernation?

Hibernation is when an animal sleeps though the winter to survive the extreme cold, and then wakes up in the spring.

Animals in hibernation do not wake up even when moved or touched.

Do frogs eat during hibernation?

During hibernation most frogs don't eat. They survive off their stored up energy.

Frogs that live on land

Frogs on land dig deep into the ground where it is warmer, or into crevices in logs and rocks to hibernate.

Frog in a log for hibernation

Frogs that live in water

To hibernate, these frogs partially bury themselves on the water's bottom, and will take oxygen from the water.

Are Frogs and Toads the Same?

Frogs and toads are two closely related species. They even grow the same way.

They both have vocal cords and lots of calls, and they also eat the same things.

African sand frog

In fact, they are pretty much the same thing, except for a few big differences.

Skin

The first thing that is very different is their skin.

Frogs have wet skin and like to live next to the water. They also have webbed feet that help them swim fast.

Tree frog in the rain

The toad's skin is dry and warty. The toad also has a rounder body, with bigger back legs.

Eggs

Another difference comes during when they lay their eggs.

Toads lay their eggs in a long chain in water that is used by many animals, and their eggs aren't very tasty to predators.

Close up of toad eggs

Frog eggs on the other hand, lay their eggs in quieter water in a patch of foam.

What Do Frogs Eat?

When frogs are first born, they can only eat plants, but as they get bigger they become carnivores.

What do most adult frogs eat?

They love to eat insects like moths and crickets and some small reptiles.

Frog eating fish in a lake

It is easy for frogs to catch insects with their long sticky tongue.

Frog catching a fly with tongue

Frogs have no teeth so they have to swallow their prey whole.

Do other animals eat frogs?

Sadly, yes. Snakes, dogs, foxes, rats, turtles and seagulls are some of the many animals that eat frogs.

A snake eating a frog

Frog Characteristics

Colors

Most frogs are green but some frogs can be yellow, brown, black, orange or red.

Tomato frog

A frog's color also helps them hide from predators.

Some frogs can even change their color to blend into the background better.

Calls

Every different kind of frog has a unique call. Certain frogs bark like a dog, while others seem to almost chirp like a bird.

Milk frog

Most frogs are calling for mates, warning off predators, or even calling for help from other frogs.

Special adaptations

Certain frog types have very special body parts, like one type of frog has sticky pads that help them stick on the grass.

Red-Eyed Tree Frog

One frog species even has small horns on their heads to protect themselves.

There are also tree frogs with very big, red eyes that they use to scare their predators away.

Blue Poison Arrow Frog

One poisonous frog species is the Blue Poison Arrow frog from Brazil.

The arrow frog lives for about 6 years in the wild.

Blue Poison Arrow Frog

The frog's feet also have suction pads on each toe, to help grip things.

They like to eat termites, ants, caterpillars and beetles.

Poison Dart Frogs

Poison Dart frogs always have brightly colored patterns in blue, black, red and yellow.

Dart frogs live in the Rainforest in Central and South America.

Poison dart frog

The poison dart frog hunts bugs and ants during the day because their brightly colored skin warns predators to stay away.

This frog's poison is on its skin, so if you every see a poison dart frog, don't touch it!

Dart frog venom is used to poison arrows for hunting.

Poison Dart frog

Scientists have discovered that the poison found on the dart frog can be used in medicine.

Tree Frogs

Tree Frogs are medium sized frogs with white stripes running down their sides.

Green Tree Frog

The female green tree frog is usually 5-7 inches long and the males are around 4-6 inches.

They eat small insects.

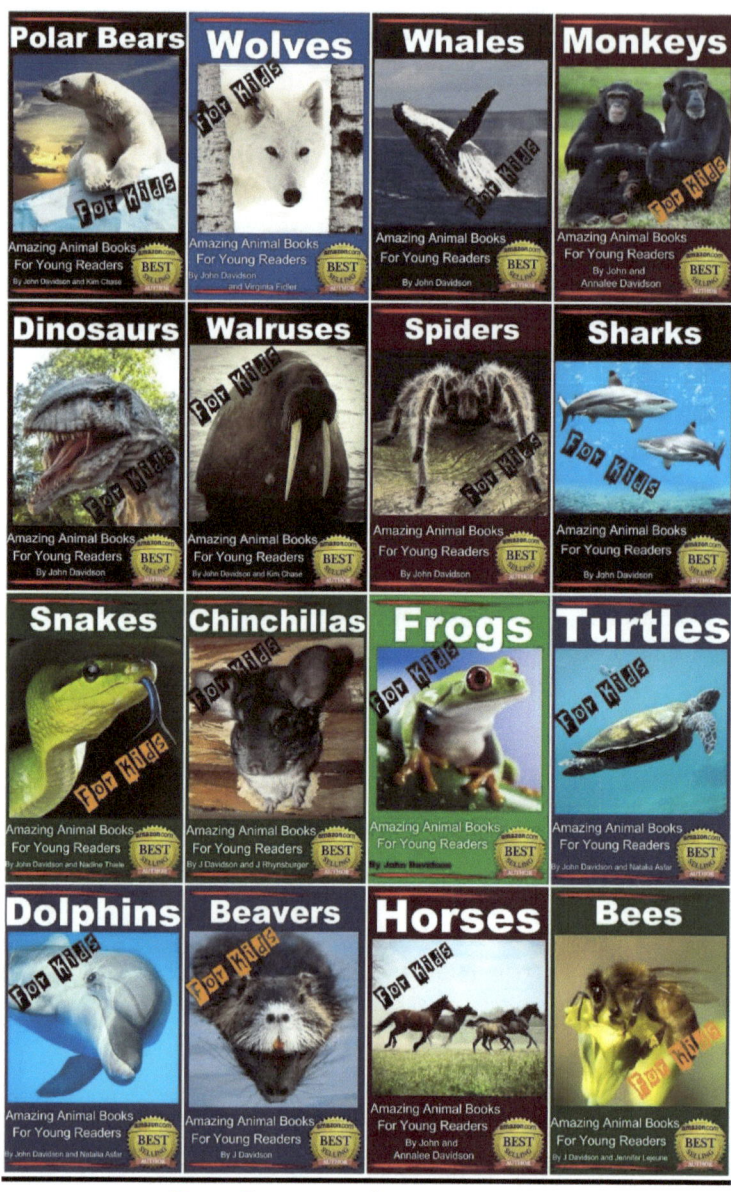

Purchase at Amazon.com

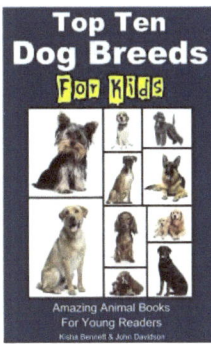

Top Ten
Dog Breeds
For Kids

Amazing Animal Books
For Young Readers
Kisha Bennett & John Davidson

German Shepherds

Dog Books for Kids
K. Bennett

Bulldogs

Dog Books for Kids
K. Bennett

Dachshund

Dog Books for Kids
K. Bennett

Poodles

Labrador
Retrievers

Dog Books for Kids
K. Bennett

Rottweilers

Dog Books for Kids
K. Bennett

Boxers

Dog Books for Kids
K. Bennett

Dog Books for Kids
K. Bennett

Golden Retrievers

Dog Books for Kids
K. Bennett

Puppies
Dog Books For Kids

AmazingAnimalBooks
By John Davidson

Beagles

Dog Books for Kids
K. Bennett

Yorkshire Terriers

Dog Books for Kids
K. Bennett

Dogs
Top Ten Dog Breeds
For Kids

Amazing Animal Books
For Young Readers
Zahra Jazeel & John Davidson

Cats
For Kids

Amazing Animal Books
For Young Readers
K. Bennett & John Davidson

Foxes
For Kids

Amazing Animal Books
For Young Readers
Zahra Jazeel & John Davidson

Wolves
For Kids

Amazing Animal Books
For Young Readers
By John Davidson and Virginia Fidler

Our books are available at

1. Amazon.com
2. Barnes and Noble
3. Itunes
4. Kobo
5. Smashwords
6. Google Play Books

Download Free Books!
http://MendonCottageBooks.com

Publisher

JD-Biz Corp

P O Box 374

Mendon, Utah 84325

http://www.jd-biz.com/

Mendon Cottage Books

P O Box 374, Mendon Utah 84325

www.ingramcontent.com/pod-product-compliance
Lightning Source LLC
Chambersburg PA
CBHW050907290526
45792CB00002B/732